Crush IT at College:

A No Nonsense Guide to Succeeding at University or College

by
Bryan Tinlin &
Danny Zacharias
© 2013

Table of Contents

Introduction...1

Part 1
What You Need To Know

1: The Secret to Getting Great Grades............................7
2: The Shocking Truth About a Bachelor of
   Arts Degree..15
3: Five Things Students Won't Do to Get
   Great Grades..25
4: 'Drop' is Not a Dirty Word—A Completely
   Different Perspective on Dropping College/
   University Courses...31
5: The Low Down on Debt—How Far In The
   Hole are You Willing to Go?............................35

Part 2
How to Crush IT

6: Crush IT at Managing Homework............................49
7: Crush IT By Arming Yourself With Skill..................57
8: Crush IT By Arming Yourself With Tools................61
9: Crush IT at Reading..69
10: Crush IT at Writing a Great Paper........................75
11: Crush IT With Productivity..................................87

Appendix: Wiping Your Grades—What to do
in the event of exceptional personal circumstances.....97

BONUS OFFER..105

Introduction
Bryan Tinlin and Danny Zacharias

This is a no nonsense guide to succeeding at university or college. If you're in higher education or thinking about it, you don't need a 200+ page book—you need practical and to-the-point advice on how to succeed, how to make the right choice, and how to Crush IT. That's what this book is about.

Students have told us over and over that they are tired of not meeting the grade expectations of post-secondary study. In fact, universities, colleges, professors, administrators, parents, and students are all saying the same thing. Why are so many students struggling and what advice can be given to help students achieve academic success?

We decided to take that challenge head on and put our experience on paper. Our goal was to write something that anyone could read in one or two sittings and we wanted to put it in plain language. We are NOT recruiting you.

Why are we qualified to write this?
We understand students because we've worked with thousands of them just like you. Danny Zacharias is a lecturer at Acadia University Nova Scotia, Canada. Bryan Tinlin has a master's degree and formerly worked as a Senior Academic Advisor with Carleton University, in Ontario, Canada. Bryan is now President of Tinlin

Academic Advising and Consulting, an independent advising service for future or current university and college students and their parents.

More than that though—between the two of us we have over 20 years of experience as university students, another 15 years teaching and advising students, and have counseled and taught over 10,000 students in our careers. We remember what it was like to make the decision of whether university or college was the right choice. We remember struggling to achieve good grades. And we both found the formula for success while we were in the thick of it. This is wisdom from the trenches.

Who Is This Book For?
Whether you have just graduated from high school and are heading to college, or you are in the midst of your studies already, this book will provide practical advice that you can put to use immediately to achieve success in your education. Whether you are a struggling student or a student who wants to get even better grades, this book will help.

What can you expect from this book?

1. Insight into student success like no other resource you'll find.
2. A practical, easy to read, guide that you can apply to your studies in order to achieve success.

3. Provides important advice to students to help them make informed decisions about their education.
4. To be challenged. At times, our advice defies conventional wisdom because it is based on real experience and training, not rumor, conjecture, urban legend, or myth.
5. Integrity. We have poured our years of experience into something we believe will be of value to you.
6. No propaganda. No college or university has paid us to write the book—you can be assured of honest advice that comes from years of experience.

We hope you enjoy our book and we look forward to hearing how you were able to Crush IT at College!

How to get in touch with us?
Danny Zacharias can be reached online at
about.me/dannyzacharias
Bryan Tinlin can be reached online at
academicadviceonline.com

Links in the Book
Numerous recommendations for apps and other items are given in the book. These are affiliate links, meaning we earn a small commission if you purchase the item using our link (we've also create shortlinks for you). If you purchase through our links, thanks very much! If you don't—no worries! We would be recommending the products no matter what.

PART 1 – What You Need To Know

Chapter 1: The Secret to Getting Great Grades
Bryan Tinlin

Do you want great grades? Most likely your answer is yes. Who says "Nah, mediocre or below average is all I'm looking for"? The real question is, have you spent more time thinking about it than actually doing it? If you were brutally honest with yourself, are you the kind of student who takes charge of your education? Do you have a "go get 'em" attitude?

If your answer is no then change that right now! You need to convince yourself that not only do you want great grades, but that you are the only one that can make it happen—because that is the cold hard truth. Once you know that you want them and that only you can get them, you ready to follow the right steps for success.

Step 1: Be in the Know
The old days of saying 'I don't' know" for just about everything are now gone. Now your answer is: 1 will find the answer. Here are a few examples to illustrate my point:

- Visit your professor during office hours to clarify lecture material and get feedback on assignments. The truth is that the bulk of academically struggling students fail to do this simple thing. If you are shy or intimidated then ask yourself: how badly do I want great grades?

- Learn your degree requirements. This is usually a major problem for most students. By taking the time to learn your requirements you will avoid taking courses that are not required for your program, thereby saving you lots of money. It also means that you can plan your schedule from year to year with some confidence.
- Get help from the writing centre and from other support services. Most students use them once they are in crisis mode and by then it's usually too late. Students avoid getting help because usually they lack interest in the course, program, or their entire studies. In short, they don't want help, otherwise they'd go and get it. That's not you because you've already committed to taking charge and to Crush IT by reading this book.

Step 2: Commit Time

Did you know that committing time to your studies is the number one way to ensure great grades? Yes, having aptitude (or the cognitive ability to comprehend and apply subject material) is important. You can't make yourself understand organic chemistry if you don't have the aptitude regardless of how much time you put in. Having said that, if you are in a program that is aligned with your aptitude (liberal arts instead of engineering if you don't have an aptitude for math for example) then you are off to the races.

How much time? Commit a minimum of two hours of study for every hour of lecture. For example, if you have 15 hours of lecture each week then you'll need to commit a minimum of 30 hours (yes 30 hours) each week of study. This is known as the 2:1 rule. It can go as high as 3:1 or 4:1 depending on how well you want to do. If you truly want great grades, commit 3:1 or 4:1. If that sounds insane, well, that's what students with great grades do. And if you are in grad school or at the doctoral level, then the 3:1 or 4:1 ratio should be all but assumed.

Step 3: Attend 100% of Your Classes!

Attending 80% of your classes isn't good enough. Attending 90% of your classes isn't good enough. If this shocks you, good! After meeting with 8,000 students I can tell you for a fact that nothing short of 100% class attendance should be acceptable in your eyes. Besides, why would you pay for something you aren't going to use? The truth is that professors cover too much material and move too quickly for you to miss any classes. Take charge and attend all of your classes.

Furthermore, if you are an auditory learner, attend a second or third time. What do I mean? Every laptop has a very good microphone on it, so record the lecture (with permission). If you want to get even more sophisticated, you can use the MS Word notebook feature which syncs the audio with your note-taking. You can do the same with an iPad app like Notability[1]

---

[1] www.tiny.cc/notability

which will sync the audio with your notes as well. If you want to get even more sophisticated and combine hand-written notes with capturing audio AND making your notes digital, purchase a LiveScribe SmartPen[2]; it syncs your hand-written notes with live audio, and then digitizes your hand-written notes and sticks them into Evernote. (Wow!)

Step 4: Commit to Your Readings

How much of the final exam do you think is based on your assigned readings? If there are only two components to a final exam, lectures and readings, then how can you expect to do well if you neglect to read 30% of your readings and 20% of your classes? Take charge and complete your readings (see the chapter on reading as well as scheduling your homework). If they are too boring to read then ask yourself, why am I in this class? If you just find it hard to read for long periods of time, you may be a strong auditory learner. Here's a tip—read out loud (make sure you are alone). Or, you can see if there is an audio version of your book. Finally, if you don't mind the robotic voice, Amazon Kindles[3] can read the text of most Kindle books for you. Computers can also do this, provided the text is in the correct format. See the chapter on reading for more tips.

Another issue students sometimes have is they don't like the repetition of class material with their textbook.

---

[2] www.tiny.cc/LivescribeSmartpen

[3] www.tiny.cc/Amazon-Kindle

While this may make the class or reading a little more boring for you, you need to simply change how you look at the situation to appreciate it. If you read a chapter from your textbook, and then the professor practically recites the chapter material (or the teacher introduces the material and then you read the chapter which is saying the same thing), then this is the PERFECT time to review and solidify the information. Take notes, make flashcards (see the Tools chapter) and think of that time as test preparation. Yes the class may not be as exciting, but choose a more positive outlook—this is more study time.

Step 5: Train like an Athlete

Many students have confessed to us that they do well on everything in their courses but their exams. There are three main reasons to explain this:

1. College and university level courses have far more weight placed on the final exam than high school classes.
2. High school students are not used to comprehensive exams, that is, where an entire term or year of material is tested.
3. Secondary school tests often use regurgitation to measure understanding whereas college and university examinations use comprehension and analysis to measure a student's understanding of the material.

As a result, many students are not properly trained for their exams from grade school. What is the trick to doing well on exams? The answer is to train like an athlete. An athlete looks at the long-term goal and establishes a routine and discipline to accomplish that goal. For a university or college student this is achieved by fulfilling these steps:

- Commit time (a minimum of 2 hours of study for every hour of lecture).
- Commit to 100% class attendance.
- Strive for 100% completion of the class readings.
- Begin to build your level of concentration to mimic an exam setting. You can't expect to concentrate during a three hour exam if you haven't trained for it. Increasing your ability to concentrate for long periods of time takes practice. Start your training early in your academic career and you will be pleasantly surprised how good of shape your brain is when it comes to the final exam.

So if you start your training in the first month of your first term of your first year, lay a solid foundation, be consistent in your work ethic, and commit to the training model, you will find yourself one step closer to academic success.

Step 6: Find a Like-Minded Peer or Mentor

Doing well isn't something you can do on your own. I know, we live in a world that values independence and in fact rewards it, but the truth is that managing things on your own is not only lonely, it also means you aren't held accountable to your commitment. All successful people have mentors. In this case, a mentor is someone who practices what they preach, is someone you can rely on, someone who cares about your academic success, and is willing to encourage you, hold your feet to the fire, and say the hard things you don't want to hear but need to. It's your job to find someone who will do this lovingly but firmly. The trick is that only you can give them permission to hold you accountable! Ask your professors for a referral if you can't find a mentor on your own.

In the end you are in charge of your education however you look at it. If you employ these 7 steps then rest assured you are on your way to Crush IT at college.

Step 7: Hang Out With Other Hard Working Students

Up until now you've probably hung out with students who do as well as you do. Or, you are hanging out with students who intend to do well but never carry it out. These 'friends' may be nice people but they may not be a positive influence on your academic record. You have two choices. Cut them off or keep them at a distance. You don't have to be rude about it and it doesn't mean they aren't your friends anymore. It just means that you are taking charge of your own academic affairs. Now, you need to zone in on the hard working students (because they usually do quite well) and befriend them. If your pride gets in the way, then you have to go back to your first objective: I will do anything to get great grades. Dave Ramsey, the financial radio guru, has a saying: if you want to be rich, do the things rich people do. To Crush IT at college, do the things "A" students do.

Chapter 2: The Shocking Truth About a Bachelor of Arts Degree
Bryan Tinlin

#1: The Purpose of a Bachelor of Arts (B.A.) is Not to Get a Job

Throughout my Academic Advising career I gave presentations to many first year classes on strategies for academic success. I also incorporated some interactive questions to keep people on their toes. One of those questions was: what is the purpose of a liberal arts education? For the few brave souls who ventured a guess, the answer was consistently, 'to get a job.' This was the same answer I received year after year. Yet interestingly enough when I asked their professors if the primary purpose of a Bachelor of Arts is to equip and prepare students for a job, their answer was always 'no.'

So what is the purpose of a Bachelor of Arts?

The primary function of a Bachelor of Arts is to teach you how to think critically. More specifically, it equips you with critical thinking, writing, reading, and research skills.

While the universities would have you believe that these skills are essential for developing the leaders of tomorrow and producing moral citizens who will make a significant contribution to society, that is only partially true. Although I agree that these critical skills are of great value in our society, these kinds of statements lead people to believe that a B.A. does in fact prepare students to move directly to the workforce.

The truth is that you are being trained by philosophers (your professors) for the purpose of becoming philosophers. Did you know that's what the "Ph" in Ph.D. stands for? Yes, that's right, 'philosophy'. Without knowing it, you've paid thousands of dollars to start your training as a philosopher.

Students spend the first four years of their undergraduate studies (or first degree) laying a foundation of theory and research. Since university is and always has been a theoretical institution, it is no wonder that this has been the focus. Unfortunately students come to university without this understanding. Should we be surprised then that four years of academic training in philosophy, theory, and research doesn't appeal to many students and consequently many fail out?

Are the critical skills taught in a BA useful in a professional career? ABSOLUTELY! Are they designed to train you for a job? No. In a nutshell, students have confused the function of a university with the function of a college. University trains students to think critically and prepares them for life as a philosopher AND to lay a firm foundation for further studies or life pursuits—both excellent things. College trains students to get a job in a particular field.

#2: The B.A. Has Major Value

This may surprise those who just read the last point, as well as all the naysayers out there. It truly is appalling to me when I hear people degrade the B.A. in an effort to convince students and recent graduates alike that the degree is of no use. Here's the good news. The B.A. is of value. It teaches highly transferable critical thinking, writing, reading, and research skills that will serve a student their entire life wherever they work and in whatever capacity they work. Employers value critical skills and so does society. You will find thousands, even millions, of people who took a B.A. in a field in which they are not currently working, nor do they intend to. But ask those same people if they valued taking their B.A. and you'll almost always get an unqualified "yes."

Several factors have conspired to devalue the B.A. in the eyes of society. To start with, people have become convinced that everyone needs a degree to be successful. Governments have fostered this belief and encouraged universities to expand their campuses at alarming rates. In order to pay for this infrastructure, more students must enroll to meet their funding targets. This has resulted in large numbers of students continuing to enroll and subsequently fail out of university when they would rather not have attended in the first place. Those who successfully graduate then enter a market already saturated with B.A. graduates. It is inevitable that many of these graduates must then work at less skilled jobs, perpetuating the perception that the degree isn't worth any more than the paper it is written on.

#3: The B.A. is Not Enough

It is unfortunate, but the reality for many students today is that a Bachelor of Arts on its own is not enough to compete in the job market. There are three reasons for this:

1. The surplus of degree holders in the marketplace has allowed employers to demand even more education from its workers. For example, although a B.A. used to be enough to secure a management level position, it is now common for many employers to ask for a graduate degree even though one may not be required. Students understand this and now commonly remark that the B.A. is worth no more than what a high school diploma once was.

2. Our economy has become knowledge-based, requiring greater levels of specialized training. This is why so many universities have partnered with trade colleges. These agreements allow a student to either earn a degree and college certification/diploma at the same time or they guarantee a certain number of credits are transferred when applying to the sister university or college.

3. Our society has become credential happy. If you aren't certified in something, you will probably struggle in the job market. Many unaccredited professions have now formed associations in the hopes of bringing greater legitimacy to their professions in the eyes of their customers.

I often recommend that students consider college training before or after completing a B.A. College training can be a wonderful complement to a university degree even if you cannot see the relevance (and vice versa). I remember explaining to a student how the skills learned in his B.A. in Economics will translate well into his career as an electrician. Did he need a B.A. to become an electrician? Certainly not, but since he had earned his degree it was important for him to understand how the critical skills acquired in his B.A. would serve him well in college and in his future career as a tradesperson.

As a final word on this subject let me say this: even if you have regrets about pursuing a B. A. instead of college, trust me, **it was not a waste**. The skills are transferable and will be with you for a lifetime.

#4: Interest is the Number One Ingredient for Success in the Arts—It is Second to None!

When I asked students what they believed to be the number one ingredient for academic success, no one ever mentioned interest. The ingredients for academic success students suggested most often were:

- strong time management skills
- hard work
- good class attendance
- good study skills
- solid organizational skills

While these are important ingredients for success, I would place them in a distant 4th place relative to the critical importance of interest.

Lack of interest is the most obvious and least discussed cause of poor academic performance. After meeting with more than 8,000 university students one-on-one at every year level and in every conceivable academic program, I would say that a lack of interest accounts for almost all academic struggles and failures. Now I'm not talking about a lack of interest in a course, program, or even degree. Students regularly make changes to their academic career to either investigate an interest or to better reflect a known interest in a particular subject. What I'm talking about is a lack of interest in studying at university.

If you think that would be uncommon, I challenge you to read the abundance of literature that point to academic disengagement. Universities across the country are establishing new research centres for student engagement, expanding student support services, hiring high-priced consultants to fix retention problems, and paying top dollar to support staff to work with students who continually struggle. Because it is impossible for the system to increase your interest, they are left with trying to fix everything else.

Universities are moving at lightning speed on this issue for two simple reasons: the first is that they are being held to a greater account today by taxpayers for the percentage of students they successfully graduate. The other reason is that the problem of academic disengagement, failing students, and ultimately drop-out rates has grown exponentially.

If you lack the kind of interest I'm referring to, my advice has always been to immediately withdraw from university studies before you invest more money (potentially sinking into more debt), and further damage your academic record. Having no interest in study and yet continuing to work on a costly degree half-heartedly is just plain stupid.

#5: A B.A. Isn't Needed To Be Successful In Life

The truth is that most students who pursue a Bachelor of Arts honestly believe, and have been conditioned to believe, that they will not be successful in life without a degree. This is simply NOT true.

Here are the top reasons students who are struggling academically report coming to university.

- I didn't know what else to do.
- I wanted to go to college but my parents said that I should come to university first (or vice versa).
- Studying X (fashion, music, drama, etc.) at a private institution wasn't practical enough for my parents. They said that I needed to go into engineering instead.
- My parents said I must. I'm the first in my family to go to university.

- My parents said I must. I come from a long line of successful professionals.
- My parents said I must. My siblings dropped out. It's all on me now.
- Society says I must.
- I was never really pressured but it was always understood that I would be going to university.
- My friends all went to university.
- It just seemed like the logical and natural thing to do.

If a degree were needed to be successful in life then trades people and other highly skilled workers must not be successful. This includes the $80+ an hour plumbers, welders, heavy duty machine operators and mechanics, carpenters, furniture makers, machinists, electricians, graphic designers, fashion consultants, and Registered Massage Therapists, just to name a few.

Now some of you may know that the trades are successful and that they are respectable professions to pursue. But at the same time you may still believe that university is better than college. This explains why participation rates at universities across the country have exploded, as have the dropout rates. Did you know 1 in every 3 students either drops out or fails to graduate after six years of study!?

Suffice it to say that a university degree isn't needed to be successful in life. There are many, many highly paid, gainfully employed college graduates who aren't saddled with $27,000 in debt like their university graduate counterparts.

Conclusion

I want to reassure those students who are already pursuing a B.A. that your degree has value and will be of value to you in your career—BUT only if you do it for the right reasons! If you lack the interest to pursue it any further, I recommend you make an immediate change and try something else. University studies are a wonderful option for those who know what they are getting themselves into, have a genuine interest in learning, are prepared to do the work and incur the cost, and are willing to invest in future educational training. If you are looking to go directly into a particular field of work, I strongly encourage you to consider college. If you don't know what you want to do, go get a job, save some money, and make a decision. Don't take the expensive university path to decide what to do with your life.

Chapter 3: Five Things Students Won't Do to Get Great Grades
Bryan Tinlin

There are loads of tips out there on how to get great grades. But what are the top recommended tips that university and college students just won't do to get great grades? Having met with over 8,000 college and university students as an Academic Advisor, here are the top five:

#1: Cancel Your Facebook Account and (Online) Gaming Subscriptions

For young women, Facebook is often the number one distraction during study time. Facebook in and of itself is a wonderful social media tool. But to young college students it is equivalent to a drink for an alcoholic. "Just 5 minutes" turns into one or two hours that were intended for schoolwork. Because Facebook is socially acceptable, many students would never fully admit that it is interfering with their ability to focus in on their studies.

For young men, gaming is a major barrier to their academic success. Unlike Facebook, few students were courageous enough to admit they were hooked on gaming. The few that admitted to it are not the only ones with the problem and I believe if you want to get great grades you need to get honest with yourself. How much of your time is stolen each week gaming?

If you truly think that you can limit your gaming, Facebook, Twitter, Pinterest, and YouTube use, then be strict with yourself. But if you recognize that you are hooked, then have the strength to get help and cut it off.

If you just need a little help with this, technology can help. Check out the Freedom app[1] which will block your internet access, or Anti-Social[2] which blocks only social media sites on Mac. Firefox users can also use the add-on LeechBlock[3] to block social media sites for periods of time.

#2: Just Say No

The bulk of the academically struggling students I met admitted that they had difficulty saying no to their friends. What's the easiest way to get into the habit of saying no to your friends? I would suggest there are three ways.

1. Say no often enough. Your 'friends' will get the message that there are only certain times in the week when you will be with them.
2. Limit your fun to one evening a week (including the weekends) and stick to it.
3. Make friends who model good study habits.

---

[1] www.macfreedom.com

[2] www.anti-social.cc

[3] www.tiny.cc/leechblock

#3: Fire Your (Distracting) Friends—At Least Until You Graduate

If you are what you eat, then you can expect your academic record to reflect whom you hang out with. Are you spending time with students who say they want to do well but don't do anything about it? These are the students who spend more time in the coffee shop, on Facebook, and going out to parties then anything academic. Firing your friends doesn't mean that you are cutting them off forever. What you are saying though is that you need to take charge of your academic decisions and hang out with students who walk the walk. In other words, you need to adopt a group of friends who have proven they have already achieved great grades. They may not be as fun as your other group but when you look at your grades at the end of the year, you'll be happy you did it!

#4: Sit at the Front of the Class

Who were the kids who sat at the front of the class in high school? The kids who wanted to listen, the smart kids. Who were the kids who sat at the back of the class in high school? To generalize they tended to be the class clowns, the delinquents and the ones who always talked. Now, which of these two groups of students do you want to be like? Keep in mind that you are forking out tens of thousands of dollars and your grades will likely determine which career doors are opened and which ones are closed.

Sitting at the front of the class has many benefits:

- It keeps you accountable. It is difficult to go unnoticed by the professor when you sit at the front.
- If you are in a class of 300 students you will actually feel like the professor is talking to you instead of at you.
- It is much easier to concentrate when you don't have row upon row of people around you on Facebook, chatting, or being otherwise distracting.

#5: Reduce Your Course Load

Like the previous four suggestions this one often gets overlooked. Reducing your course load can pay off for many students but there are three distinct groups of students who will find it particularly advantageous.

Personal Difficulties

The first group includes students who have some sort of personal difficulty impacting their ability to commit to a full course load. Examples of personal difficulties include: illness, family illness, death in the family, financial struggles, learning disability, or a hurt, habit, or hang-up that hasn't been dealt with (e.g. compulsions, addictions and obsessive behaviors).

Working More Than 15 Hours a Week at a P/T Job

The second group includes students who work more than 15 hours at a part-time job. To do well academically students should commit a minimum of two hours of study for every hour of lecture—at the grad level (i.e. for a masters degree) it is three hours. Ordinarily a full-time student in the liberal arts has about 15 hours of lecture. Applying the 2:1 rule means they should be committing a minimum of 30 hours of study or 45 hours a week in total. If a student were to work 25 hours at a part-time job then they would be attempting 70 hours a week between work and school. So, if you work more than 15 hours a week, reduce your course load to allow yourself to commit a minimum of 2:1 each week.

Course Load is Too Heavy
The third group is made up of students who can't handle a 100% course load. To be clear, if you fall into this category you are:

- wise, not a fool
- intelligent, not unintelligent
- courageous, not lazy.

If you are on a scholarship and need to stay as a full-time student, work with an advisor to see if some courses can be moved to the summer. If you feel your load is too heavy but want to stay with it, then you need to cut out other things in your life (part-time work, volunteer time, dating, etc) and buckle down. There are only so many hours in a week.

In my experience, I've never heard a single regret from a student who took longer to complete their degree and got great grades—but I have heard countless regrets from students who recorded low grades because they took on too much. Remember, in the end it doesn't matter how long it takes you to complete your program but rather how well you did.

Chapter 4: 'Drop' is not a Dirty Word – A Completely Different Perspective on Dropping College/University Courses
Bryan Tinlin

There are three solid reasons why dropping a course is not something to be fearful of and can in certain circumstances be the wisest choice you can make! Had I been given this advice when I was a first year student, I would have saved myself from three D's on my permanent academic record. Now they are with me forever.

Consider this: you are in a first year course where the mid-term is worth 50% of your grade and the final exam is worth 50% of your grade. On the mid-term, you barely pass by getting 25 of the possible 50 points. That means you'll need a perfect grade (all 50 points) on your final exam just to get a B or 75% grade in the end. How realistic is that when you have missed a number of classes, are behind in the readings, and have lost track of most of what was said in class?

Given the scenario above, why would a student contemplate 'sticking it out'? In my 8,000 sessions with students, here's what they have told me:

- Dropping is like quitting and I'm not a quitter.
- I need this course for my program.
- If I don't complete this course it will screw up my schedule next year.
- It's only my first year. It really doesn't matter.

- My parents would be furious if they knew I dropped it.
- If I withdraw, a 'W' will appear on my permanent record (i.e. my transcript).

It all boils down to a fear of failure.

Here is the reality: A low grade in one course will not likely ruin you academically. The question is, how many other low grades are you racking up this year? As an Academic Advisor, I almost always encouraged students to drop in this scenario. Here are three reasons why:

1: Lay a Solid Foundation for Your Future

It's hard to do well in subsequent courses when you haven't laid a solid foundation in first and second year courses. Who cares, you ask? Well, think of it like building a house. If your foundation is weak, the rest of your house will be too. Trust me when I say that solid skills early on will bring success later.

2: Think long Term—Your future Career is at Stake

Are you looking for an even more compelling reason than laying a solid foundation? How about maintaining a solid academic record? If I had a dime for every student who said they wanted to go on to professional studies (like law or medicine) or some other profession that required outstanding grades throughout their studies, I'd be rich. Again, a low grade is not the end of your academic career, but your goal should be making the best decisions you can now for your future.

3: Get the Facts First, Then Make a Decision

Some institutions assign a 'W' for withdrawal when students drop courses. Many students believe this is a punitive notation and will adversely affect their permanent record. This is not true, since the withdrawal does not explain why the student dropped the course. You may have dropped it for any number of compelling reasons including: illness, personal struggles, or financial difficulties. In fact, you may have exercised great wisdom in dropping the course realizing that you were way in over your head.

The point is that you have a choice between recording a potentially low grade on your permanent academic record and instead take a 'W' which does not affect your Grade Point Average (GPA), assuming your institution even assigns one. There are consequences for low grades, but no consequences for withdrawals. Consider this the next time you are faced with the decision to drop or not to drop.

Finally, it is important to understand that dropping is not quitting. In fact, knowing when to fold 'em (like the country song says) is a sign of maturity and wisdom.

Chapter 5: The Low Down on Debt – How Far In The Hole Are You Willing To Go?
Bryan Tinlin

One of the greatest stressors for students is the amount of debt they will accumulate over the course of their studies. But there are many ways to minimize your debt and be a better steward of the money you have either saved or borrowed. We should know, as both of us authors racked up over 30k in debt because we made bad choices. If we had exercised a little more common sense we could likely have had money sitting in our bank accounts at the end of our respective degrees.

Here are 12 tips to help you to stay debt free or significantly reduce your total debt upon graduation.

#1: Pay for Courses When You Can Afford Them

One of the best ways to avoid student debt is to pay for courses as you can afford them. Many students overlook this option for three reasons:

1. It will take you longer to complete your studies.
2. It can be frustrating to have to put your future career on hold.
3. The perceived loss of income – the money you would have otherwise earned had you completed your studies on a full-time basis.

While there are advantages to completing a program on a full-time basis, there is also the reality of the interest you will have to pay on the total debt. In the end, it becomes a cost-benefit analysis for each student. There's no question that pursuing courses as you can afford them will leave you debt free or with a significantly reduced debt load.

Balancing work and school is more important than you may think. In an effort to graduate debt free and complete their program in a normal time frame, many students make the mistake of working too many hours while maintaining a high course load. This often has dire consequences. The most notable consequence is the rate at which students burn out. Burnout can result in poor academic performance, even failure, and consequently the need to repeat courses. In many cases, students pay to repeat failed courses by working as many or even more hours than they were before. This cycle often continues until graduation.

In the end, these students graduate debt free but they have also:

- worked far more hours and paid more tuition while failing and recording many low grades because of a lack of balance between work and school
- compromised the integrity of their academic record and unintentionally limited their admission to professional and graduate studies
- put their mental and physical health at risk

Students who decide to work while attending school need to accept the possibility of taking longer to complete their program while maintaining their academic record, their bank account and their mental health.

#2: Seek out Scholarships and Bursaries

There are two categories of financial assistance offered through a college or university: scholarships and bursaries.

Entrance Scholarships

Entrance scholarships are based on academic merit. The higher your grades entering college or university, the more money you will receive. Many students are considered for scholarships automatically when they apply to a college or university while other scholarships require that you submit an application.

In-Course Scholarships

These are scholarships a student can receive as they progress through their academic program. Again, the higher the grades you achieve the more money you will receive. Most in-course scholarships, including the dean's list, are awarded automatically.

Transfer Scholarships

Transfer scholarships are available to students coming from a community college to a university or from one university to another. If the institution you intend to apply to offers transfer scholarships then it is certainly worthwhile to submit an application if one is required.

Bursaries
Bursaries, like loans, are based on financial need. The chief difference is that bursaries do not need to be repaid. It is also important to keep in mind that students who have submitted and qualify for government financial assistance are more likely to qualify for bursaries since the two are often linked.

Whatever your financial position, it is always wise to spend a fair amount of time on the financial aid web site of your college or university. This is one of the major sources of revenue students often overlook as part of their financial planning for diploma or degree studies.

Parents and Grandparents
Your family may or may not be able to assist you, but if they can, then be sure to honor that pledge by working your butt off. Sometimes your parents or grandparents need to be asked. If this is the case, do so humbly and be sure you completely understand if they cannot— remember, they don't owe you anything and are under no obligation to help you. But remember, if you follow all of these tips, then even $20 a month from some family members will help you.

One tip when talking to family: be sure that you pledge to pay it forward. Tell your family that you promise to do the same thing for other family members in the future.

#3: Avoid Buying a Car
Parking, gas, maintenance, insurance, and repairs all add to student debt. Unless you absolutely need a car

(which means there is NO way to commute or take public transit) it is highly recommended you avoid a car at all costs. There isn't a single extravagant expense that cripples the financial life of a student more than a car. Even if someone is willing to buy you a car while you are studying, the monthly payments are not worth it. Here are your alternatives:

- Find a job closer to school – this will save you from having to work to pay for your car.
- Live closer to school.
- Walk or take transit.
- Hitch a ride with friends who aren't as smart as you and want to spend their money on a car.

#4: Be Smart With the Technology You Purchase

Although it is nice to have the latest and greatest technology, think carefully before diving in. Is buying a laptop a good investment in your education? Absolutely. Is a smart phone a wise investment? Absolutely not! The service fees alone will add to your student debt very quickly and it is difficult to get out of a contract once you commit. In the end ask yourself which is most important: reducing your debt or having the convenience of technology you want but really don't need. If you really feel you need a cell phone for safety, find an old phone and buy a pre-paid card. Remember too that most campuses are entirely wireless today—you can use apps like MagicJack on an iPod (not iPhone) or an Android device to call any North American number for free over WiFi.

#5: Pack Your Lunch

Colleges and universities make a fortune selling you food, coffee, pastries, and just about everything else. You'll save yourself a pile of money if you follow three simple tips:

- Pack your lunches and snacks.
- Make your own dinner.
- Bring a thermos of your own favorite coffee or tea—that daily Starbucks Grande coffee price could pay for a whole course!
- STOP going out to eat. If you must, make it a once a month thing.

Your friends will think you are frugal and guess what? They're right. The only difference is you will be the one saving hundreds of dollars every single month, and you won't be crawling out of debt for years post-graduation like everyone else!

#6: Find a Bunk Mate

Well you may not have to go quite that far, but it certainly can save you a lot of money if you were to share accommodation expenses with some friends. Find out the electricity and heating bills prior to moving in with your friends. This information is available from the utility commission or even the landlord if you ask. In some cases, you may find that the relatively high utility bills and your share of the rent make it a poor financial decision. Crunch the numbers so you have an idea what your expenses will be. You are just one person, you don't need a lot. Find the cheapest possible place to live.

Sometimes living in dorm is the best option, but that is not always the case.

Another option that many students resist is staying home. It is understandable that many students after high school want to move out and have their freedom. But if you're serious about staying out of debt and you can stay home, do it. Most parents will not charge you rent if you are studying. Plus, you may get the added bonus of meals prepared for you, clothes washed for you, etc.

#7: Say No To Alcohol

If you are determined to minimize your debt then you'd be wise to give up alcohol. Students consume booze at a rate that keeps bar owners flush with cash. Saying no to alcohol means saying no to debt. If you don't feel like you can go that far, then try going out with only your ID and a $10 bill—don't give yourself the chance to use debit or credit. And if the party is at home, don't be the one to offer to pick up the alcohol. Give them that $10 bill and let them pay any extra.

#8: Say No to Mexico and Yes to Study Week

Ah yes, the tantalizing trip south. While it is true that your friends may return with a nice tan, they will also have paid the high price for their week-long stint on the beach. Consider the many benefits of saying no to a spring break holiday down south:

1. You will have avoided adding to your total debt load.
2. You can actually save money by continuing to work at your part-time job while your friends are on the beach spending their borrowed money.
3. You will have invested time in your studies. In high school, the trip to sunny climates landed on March Break. At university or college the same trip lands on reading week or study week. Get the point? When your friends are stressed to the max because they took time to soak in the sun pretending to read, you will be at ease because you were actually reading and preparing for the end of the academic term.

Is it fun to say no to a sunny vacation? Of course not! But you will be richer and smarter because of the wise choice you made. And think of the fun you will have on a real vacation once you graduate, have a job to pay for it, aren't a slave to your debt, and no longer have to worry about all the studying you should be doing.

#9: Rent Month by Month

Many students choose to return home to their parents for the summer in order to earn money for next year's tuition. Unfortunately if you have signed a year-long lease then you're stuck paying for an apartment, and perhaps trying to find a subletor for the remaining months (like every other student around you!). Short of finding a reliable person to sublet your apartment, you will spend a good chunk of your summer's earning on rent that could have otherwise been saved for next year.

Try to find accommodation with a flexible rental agreement that works with your academic school year. The best kind of agreement is always month-by-month. If the landlord really wants a year-long agreement, see if you can negotiate a slightly higher monthly payment for an 8 or 9 month contract.

#10: Beware of Your Financial Drop Deadlines
Every college or university has drop deadlines. In fact, there are usually two distinct deadlines: academic and financial. Academic deadlines ensure that no academic penalty is applied to your permanent record if you drop a course(s) by the deadline.

Financial drop deadlines are equally important, although a little more complicated, and usually occur in the first four weeks of each semester. Many schools will offer either:

- A prorated refund – the longer you wait to drop the course the lower the refund, OR
- an all or nothing refund – Many schools are moving to option #2. The key is to abide by the deadline. If you drop the course(s) by the financial drop deadline you will be entitled to a 100% refund. Failure to drop the course by the financial drop deadline results in a 0% refund.

Pay careful attention to the refund policy. Some institutions apply a flat rate for full-time tuition regardless of course load. For instance, a student might pay the same price for an 80% course load as a student taking a 90% course load. In this scenario only when a student drops below an 80% course load is he/she entitled to a full refund, provided the course is dropped by the financial drop deadline. Check with your institution to find out if they have a flat rate.

#11: Community College is far Cheaper than a University Degree

If you want to get a great education but don't want to spend your life in debt then community college is a great option. A diploma or certificate program at a local community college is far less expensive than a full-fledged university degree and will take you half the time to earn it. The major advantage of community college is that you will be equipped with job ready skills and, if you've made a wise choice, you are likely to earn a good wage as soon as you graduate.

This is not to say that a university degree is an unwise choice! (See the Shocking Truth chapter). BUT if you are unclear on what you are even trying to get out of higher education, don't take the expensive road while deciding!

#12: Go Back to The Future

This is probably the most difficult tip to put into practice, but also the most important because it is more than just a practice; it is a mindset. You need to close your eyes and fast-forward your life 3 to 5 years. You will either graduate and charge out into the workforce with little to no debt (something you can pay off in a year), or, along with most of your peers, you will be drowning in debt for 5 or more years. Student loans don't feel real when you are getting free money, but when you are being asked to pay anywhere from $300-$1,000 a month you will soon be an adult asking your grandma if you can live in her basement. Your life will be on hold as you are in bondage to your debt. If I could go back in time, I would punch myself in the face and tell myself to wise up. I would tell myself to pay my own way with a job rather than rely on student loans. And I would tell myself to live more frugally. I'm intent on helping as many students as possible learn from MY mistake.

The Long-term Consequences of Debt

The consequences of student debt don't always hit home until student loan or credit card statements arrive at your door or in your email 'Inbox'. Only then are you required to face the true cost of the decisions you made during those years of academic study. Here are just a few additional costs you incur while paying off your debt:

- Potential savings go towards loan repayment.
- Inability to accept jobs you really want or need for career experience because they don't pay enough to cover your debt repayment and living expenses.

- Difficulty finding additional money to save for your first home or car.
- Paying your landlord's mortgage through rent payments instead of building equity for yourself through a mortgage.
- Poor credit rating if your payments aren't on time.
- The overall drain on your financial resources, specifically money for the fun stuff.
- The potential to get further into debt in order to live while repaying student debt.

Conclusion

In the end, the amount of debt you incur is largely determined by the choices you make. You may not be willing to take all of the steps to be completely debt free, but by making wise decisions and frugal choices you can cut your debt repayment by many years. Choices today will save you money and afford you choices tomorrow. You will either listen to the advice in this chapter and be unique among your peers, or in 4 or 5 years, you will wish you had listened.

PART 2 – How to Crush IT

Chapter 6: Crush IT at Managing Homework
Danny Zacharias

I've been a student for a long time. Through my undergrad, I wasn't great at managing my life. But going through my two masters degrees, I got to the point that I was no longer pulling all-nighters, or working frantically all weekend. No one taught me how to go into my semesters with a plan, but if you want to survive and thrive, you need one. The key is making a plan and sticking to it. Follows these steps to plan out your semester in the first week and stick to it.

Step 1: Process Your Syllabi

Once you begin receiving your syllabi for the classes you're taking, you need to begin to process them into your master plan of action. This will OVERWHELM you— but it is better to feel overwhelmed at the beginning rather than the end, trust me! Find all of the due dates on each syllabus and circle them. For

> **The 3 Labels**
>
> The *major assignments* label is any project that has a lot of marks associated with it. Essays, tests, exams, presentations, etc., usually fall under this category.
>
> The *minor assignments* label is for projects worth few marks and that won't take you more than a few hours, at most a day, to complete.
>
> The *reading label* is for any required reading for your classes.

each assignment or test label them using these 3 labels: reading, minor assignments, major assignments.

A suggestion—if there are presentations for a class and you can choose a date, grab one of the first 3 available slots as soon as you can, i.e. give yourself an early date. I even would approach my professor after the very first class. Don't make the mistake of choosing to do a presentation in the last week of the semester when everything else is due.

Step 2: Set Your Calendar/Homework Manager For the Semester

Now take every due date from your syllabi and put it into your calendar/homework manager of choice (see the Tools chapter). As you put the due dates in for your major and minor assignments, keep in mind that you should try to complete minor assignments 1 day before they are due, and major assignments 5-7 days before. If you want to stay on top of things, create this additional "have done by" due date for each assignment. Think about it—If you can finish a major paper, and ignore it for a few days, and then proofread it a few days before it is due, you will find all sorts of mistakes that you will be able to clean up before handing in. Also, these early dates will provide margin for your life. When your dear old aunt Betty dies and three days of your life are consumed, you need to have some margin in your life so that these circumstances don't cause major problems at school. Planning ahead will help your life from getting derailed by unforeseen circumstances.

You also need to add your class times, labs, tutorials, work shifts, volunteer time, exercise, etc., into your calendar. When you are a university student, school is your full-time job, so treat it as such. Planning this out will ensure that you are prepared for that all-weekend camp trip with your friends, rather than realizing the night before that you have a major assignment due on Monday. Trust me that assignment will not get done!

Now here is the really important part of this step—add blocks of study time to your schedule. These will be the times when you get all of those assignments and readings done. If you have a class in the morning, then the afternoon should be study time. If you have a whole weekday with no class, get up along with the other students for 8:30 and find a place in the library. Your class time and study blocks should add up to anywhere between 40-60 hours per week.

Example Week Schedule

	Sat	Sun	Mon	Tue	Wed	Thu	Fri
Morning	optional study	Church	Psych class	Study	Study	Chem class •item due •item due	Study
Afternoon	Study	optional study	Study	Bio class •item due	English class	Econ class •item due	Study
Evening	P/T Job		P/T Job	Study	Study		P/T Job

Study Time

READING
☐ Bio text ch.5 (due Tue)
☐ Hamlet (due next Wed)
☐ Chem text ch.3 (due Thu)
☐ Econ text ch.4 (due Thu)
☐ Psych text ch.3 (due next Mon)

MINOR
☐ Chem assignment (due Fri)
☐ Bio Assignment (due next week)

MAJOR
☐ Econ Presentation (due next week)
☐ Bio text (due in 2 weeks)

Step 3: Work the Plan and Adjust Each Week

Now that you have slaved over your syllabi and got them into your calendar system and put into your calendar other events that you are committed to (work included), you need to lay out what you'll be doing every single week of your semester and stick to it. Every week you should be working on items under the three labels: you will have a weekly reading schedule, small assignments to finish, and major assignments to work on. For a typical schedule you will be working on 1-4 minor assignments each week, and 1 or 2 major assignments each week. It may be that a particular minor project goes by a lot quicker than the time you have allotted. This will give your schedule some flexibility for 1) those times when minor projects take a little more time than you thought, 2) will provide more time for working on your major projects, 3) will allow you to bring next week's assignments forward to this week so that you are ahead of the game. I don't know why, but students often think that a syllabus dictates when you should work on a particular assignment! your syllabus does not say "start this assignment that is worth 50% of your grade 2 days before the due date."

Take control of your own life and own it. By the end of your first week of class you should begin working on a major project, even if it is not due until the last day of class. So every day on your calendar there should be no wondering what to do—do your reading then do your minor assignment(s), then do your major assignment. And keep an eye on your master plan. Review it daily and weekly. A close due date always takes priority over everything else.

If you work this plan and find that you cannot keep up or too many of your assignments are being brought forward to the next week, several things might be happening:

1. You may be taking too much time on your reading and small assignments. Remember to read actively (see the reading chapter) and don't distract yourself with time-wasters.
2. Ask yourself if you are REALLY putting in the time. Are you working hard and being productive and efficient, or are you working for 15 minutes, then checking Facebook, then reading for 5 minutes, then chatting for 10 minutes, then texting someone, then working for 15 minutes, etc.
3. If you feel you are honestly putting in the time, working efficiently, and not procrastinating, then you need to start thinking seriously about dropping something. It may be one less work shift or one less class (see the Drop chapter).

The next thing you will need to do on a week-by-week basis, particularly if you have a part-time job or volunteer, is adjust your weekly schedule. But the beauty of blocking time for homework is that those blocks can move around to fit and adjust to your schedule. Following this plan and treating your studies like your full-time job will also make unexpected events less stressful for you because if you follow this plan you will often be 1-3 weeks ahead of your peers. Take control of your time, be ruthless about your schedule, and you will Crush IT.

Chapter 7: Crush IT By Arming Yourself With Skills
Danny Zacharias

The old saying that 'a carpenter is only as good as his tools' is a truism for all of life. Think about professional golfers. They arm themselves with top-notch clubs and gear. But more than that, they work hard to learn how to use those tools to the best of their ability. Like any pro out there, they practice their craft.

For your life as a student, you need to arm yourself in order to be successful. Arming yourself comes on two fronts—your skills and your tools. Learn a few core skills, and you will Crush IT at college. Have some good tools (and know how to use them) and you'll be the envy of your fellow students. This chapter is about skills, the next is about tools.

Skill 1: Know the Library

Every paper you write should involve at least one trip to the library. Don't be one of those foolish students who only access what they can find online (usually out of laziness). Aim for the best, not the most convenient.

The library is a big place, and you are wise to take some time to get to know and understand how everything works. During your orientation week you may receive a library tour - but after that, during your first weeks into the semester, get an appointment with someone at the library. Get them to explain to you the online catalog system. Ask them how to access online journal articles. Ask what the process is for getting something your library may not have. A not-insignificant portion of your tuition goes towards the library—it is meant to be a huge reservoir of resources for you. So get the training to make use of it!

Skill 2: Research

Very closely related to your library skills are your research skills. Large libraries typically have specialized librarians for particular areas of research. Seek these people out when you are ready to launch into your first essay in a particular field. Ask them how to find good resources on a topic, and find out what online database(s) you should use when looking for good resources. These people are there to help you. Your tuition is paying some of their salary, so make use of them!

Skill 3: Writing

Most degrees require written assignments and essays. Some may require technical reports. Even if you are pursuing a certificate at a college and you are not at a university, there is a right way and a wrong way to do your assignments. Don't assume that the writing skills you have from high school are going to cut it anymore...it is time to kick it up a notch!

As soon as you begin a class, be sure to understand thoroughly what the teacher is looking for, especially if the syllabus is not very specific. Ask your professor if they have an example you can see. If that fails, ask if they have a TA (teaching assistant) you can meet with over lunch to discuss assignments.

If you are working on a B.A., essay writing is almost always required. But don't think that this needs to be a solo effort. Most universities have a writing help centre, or tutors for writing. Take every advantage of these so that you can learn how to write academically. Have your first few essays done well in advance so that you can go over the whole thing with a tutor. Grammar, spelling, punctuation, formatting, clarity—all of this matters, so don't be sloppy!

Skill 4: Citing

Citation is the method by which you indicate what books or articles you are quoting or making use of. Professors always want you to properly cite sources that you use in an assignment. It may seem tedious (and it sometimes is) but do not neglect it. Improper citation can significantly drop your mark on a paper. Failing to cite something at all when you use quotations or ideas...this is plagiarism and you may be ejected from the course or from the school!

There are several styles of citation. Be sure to find out on your syllabus what method of citation your professor wants, and if it isn't specified then ask directly. Both a writing tutor and your school's librarian can help you find the right resources for learning proper citation.

This skill can also greatly improve if you use the right kind of tools (see the Tools chapter).

Skill 5: Presentation

You will eventually have to present in front of your class and professor—so impress them all! Make slides (with Powerpoint[1] or Keynote[2], or Prezi[3]) that are engaging, with nice photos and not too much text. Prepare some handouts for the class, and practice what you are going to say beforehand. Be the kind of presenter you would like to listen to: don't just read a prepared statement with no eye contact and filled with "um," "uh," and "like." Be engaging. Your aim is to impress every person in the room with what you say and how you said it. If you have a classmate you don't know say to you "that was really good," or "thanks I learned a lot," or "I enjoy listening to you more than the professor" then you know you've done well! Yes, your peers will tell you. I've received all of these complements while a student!

Train yourself with the right skills, practice and refine, and go Crush IT.

_____

[1] www.tiny.cc/PowerpointApp

[2] www.tiny.cc/KeynoteApp

[3] www.prezi.com

Chapter 8: Crush IT By Arming Yourself With Tools
Danny Zacharias

Tool 1: Calendar / Scheduler

If you want to be in command of your life during your higher education years, then you need to be in control of your time. The particulars of how to schedule your semesters were dealt with in Chapter 6, but suffice it to say that you need to get used to using a good calendar. If you have a Mac, you already have one built in. If you use a PC and bought MS Office, you have Outlook. If you prefer an online version, Google Calendar is great.

If you want an option that is a little more specific to homework management, there are some good options too. iProcrastinate is a good Mac[4] & iOS[5] option, as is iStudiez Pro (Mac[6] & iOS[7]). Finally, soshiku.com is a great online option that can be accessed on mobile devices as well.

Tool 2: Word Processor

I am constantly surprised at how many people don't know or can't figure out how to use their word processor (usually Microsoft Word)—even office people who do most of their work with it! Don't be one of those people.

---

[4] www.tiny.cc/iProcrastinateMac

[5] www.tiny.cc/iProcrastinateiOS

[6] www.tiny.cc/iStudiezMac

[7] www.tiny.cc/iStudieziOS

You shouldn't have to wrestle with your word processor at 3 am to get the page numbers right! Instead, be intentional and learn how to use it in advance. Not only can you use the help files, but turn to YouTube for video tutorials when you need more help.

While Microsoft Word tends to be the standard word processor, it can be a bit much as it is made to do everything under the sun. If you are a Mac user, iWork Pages[8] is a very nice word processor to use. If you are looking for free, OpenOffice[9] will do everything you need it to. And don't forget Google Docs[10], a free online option that can do pretty much everything you need it to as well.

Whatever word processor you decide on (there are many others), be sure you know from memory how to do at least these things:

- spellcheck (You have ZERO excuse for spelling mistakes with the technology you have today!)
- page numbering - including how to use section breaks for restarting page numbers
- adding to your headers and footers
- creating columns (section breaks can be important here too)
- line-spacing
- how to add a footnote or endnote

---

[8] www.tiny.cc/iWorkPages

[9] openoffice.org

[10] docs.google.com

If you are involved in more advanced studies where you are writing larger pieces of work (like a thesis), then you should also become familiar with paragraph styles—how to alter them and use them effectively. This will save you a lot of time.

Tool 3: Note-taking System

In the reading chapter, note-taking will be discussed. It is a VERY good idea to keep all of your notes in the same place or system. I also recommend going electronic

> "A pen is a mental crowbar"
> —Howard Hendricks

with your notes. I know some people like pen and paper, but the truth of the matter is that electronic notes are much more handy. and useful to you They can be searched, added to, copied and pasted. And the great thing about note-taking systems today is that they do so much more than just keep your notes—they are databases for you to store whatever you want. These programs make it easy for you to capture webpages, store PDFs, etc. These programs are digital filing cabinets.

There are many options to choose from today. If you own a PC, you may already have Microsoft OneNote[11] installed. For Mac users, DEVONthink[12] is a powerful

---

[11] www.tiny.cc/OneNote

[12] www.tiny.cc/Devonthink

database. For Mac[13] (and iOS[14]) CP Notebook is a beautiful interface that replicates a notebook style. By far the most popular note-taking and database system is Evernote.[15] Evernote is cross-platform, mobile, and free up to a certain storage amount. Whatever you choose, become a guru for that software. Watch video tutorials, access the help files, and read the fantastic Evernote Essentials[16] if Evernote is your choice.

Lastly, I recommended digital note-taking and I hold firm to that. But did you know that you can hand-write your notes and digitize them? What's more, you can sync a live audio lecture with your notes! If this sounds like what you need, then purchase a LiveScribe SmartPen[17]; it syncs your hand-written notes with live audio, and then digitizes your hand-written notes and sticks them into Evernote.

Tool 4: Flashcards

The use of good old flashcards is still one of the best ways to memorize large amounts of information. Fortunately for you, flashcards have also gone digital, so you don't need to carry around wads of cards, you can access them on your computer or mobile device. What's

---

[13] www.tiny.cc/NoteBookMac

[14] www.tiny.cc/NotebookiOS

[15] www.evernote.com

[16] www.tiny.cc/EvernoteEssentials

[17] www.tiny.cc/LivescribeSmartpen

more, many times you won't even need to make the cards! Quizlet.com is a fantastic and free online resource for the exchanging of flashcards. Odds are that the textbook you'll be quizzed on already has a set of flashcards that someone else has made that you can make use of. Quizlet can be used online and on mobile devices. If you use a Mac or iOS device and are looking for a bit nicer of an interface, Mental Case (Mac[18] or iOS[19]) is a superb flashcard app—and you can still make use of the Quizlet databases within Mental Case. Making regular use of flashcards for study will help you absorb all of that information, and having them on your mobile device means you can study anywhere conveniently.

Tool 5: Citation Software

Learning how to cite properly was listed as Skill 4 in the previous chapter. There are, thankfully, numerous tools to help you cite properly. I was still in college at the advent of citation tools. Prior to finding this type of software, I would spend just as much time on my footnotes and bibliography as the research and writing! Working on proper citation is painful. But when someone introduced me to software tools that could properly format my footnotes and bibliography, I saw the potential and immediately became a guru of citation software. If you are doing a lot of writing and a lot of citing—you should too.

---

[18] www.tiny.cc/MentalCaseMac

[19] www.tiny.cc/MentalCaseiOS

The most basic citation software is built right into the latest versions of Microsoft Word. A more advanced option that still works within MS Word is EazyPaper.[20] These items will ask you to put the information in for a book or article, and it will properly format your footnotes and bibliography (again, BE SURE to find out what citation style your professor wants).

If you are only writing a limited amount of essays, the above recommendations will serve you well. However, if you are specializing in an area in which you will be writing a lot of essays, or especially if you are a grad student or Doctoral student, you owe it to yourself to start using bibliographic management software. As a professor and academic, my bibliographic manager is one of the top tools in my toolbox. Not only will it save you HOURS by formatting your citations and bibliography correctly, but it will also be a place where you can store your articles and reading notes in a searchable database.

Students have numerous options from which to choose. The most well-known bibliographic manager (Mac or PC) is Endnote—but it is also the most pricy. An affordable cross-platform option is Papers[21]—good especially for the sciences. An affordable option for PC is Biblioscape,[22] and an affordable Mac option is

---

[20] www.eazypaper.com

[21] www.papersapp.com

[22] www.biblioscape.com

Bookends.[23] For students on a budget, there are some popular and very good free options too. Mendeley [24] (cross platform) and Sente[25] (Mac, and my tool of choice) are both free and sync to the cloud so you'll never lose your information, plus you can highlight and mark up PDF's directly in the software. Both of these free options are also scalable in that you can pay for an increased amount of cloud storage.

Tool 6: {Insert Tool Here}

I have tried to be as broad in my tool choices as possible, but the truth is that there are many more tools that could be listed that are more specific to certain disciplines and trades. There is autoCAD for designers, Photoshop for photography, Logos for theology, SPSS for sociology, etc. The list can go on and on.

Here is what you need to take away: become a master of that tool. You need to become a guru for that software. You want your peers to refer to you as the walking manual on that tool. Whatever tool it is, whether software, hardware, gadgets, or actual carpenter tools, wield it with perfection. Know how to do every cool little thing; memorize as many of the keyboard shortcuts as you can; and know where to go if you don't know something.

---

[23] www.tiny.cc/Bookends

[24] www.mendeley.com

[25] www.thirdstreetsoftware.com

Conclusion

Unless you are an older college student, you are fairly comfortable with technology, particularly for social aspects of the internet. But now is the time to tap into the power of your laptop for your education and learn how to use tools that will help you Crush IT.

Chapter 9: Crush IT at Reading
Danny Zacharias

Different Kinds of Reading
It may seem odd to think that there are different kinds of reading. Isn't reading that thing we all do with words on a page or screen?

Well—yes and no. When you are studying, especially in higher education, you will be reading A LOT. But you should NOT be reading the same way you just finished reading your last engrossing novel. You read a novel curled up on your sofa with a blanket and a warm drink. You read it from beginning to end, in that order. You are reading for the sheer delight and entertainment of reading.

Don't read your textbooks and your research materials like that. Don't curl up on the couch. Don't read from beginning to end. And while you (hopefully) will enjoy learning, this isn't entertainment reading. Reading for learning is different. It is an active exercise for information extraction.

I had a teacher once who referred to his books as friends that he had conversations with. I always loved that analogy and it has stuck with me. For you, think of textbook and essay authors as teachers, because after all, they will be teaching you something. And there are some things about these hundreds of teachers that are EVEN better than live teachers:

- They (usually) stay on topic.

- They don't let others interrupt their train of thought.
- Like TiVo, you can rewind and fast-forward their discussion. You can pause them, go back to listen one more time to what they said, and even check out the ending first.

As you come to one of these new teachers, come with the purpose of understanding their arguments and information—not for entertainment. Here are things to do and keep in mind when reading.

Be An Active Reader

Sit up while you are reading, and have a pen and paper or your laptop nearby to take notes. You are reading for information, so work to extract that information. And here is a simple little tip: you can easily double your reading speed by simply using a pen or your finger to go back and forth on the page. That pointer forces you to stay at a good pace. Trust me, it works!

Reading requires your attention (duh!). That may seem obvious, and yet you will be prone to watch something on your laptop, listen to your latest album purchase, be text messaging, or have a conversation. This won't work, and you know it won't work—so don't fool yourself. Stick on some music, but make it instrumental and quiet. Turn off your messaging service. Turn off your email. And read somewhere you won't be interrupted by friends.

Decide If It Is Worth Reading

Not every item you come across is worth reading. The key is being able to quickly decide if it is worth reading or not. For instance, your assigned textbooks should be read thoroughly in the order your professor suggests, because in choosing that textbook he/she is telling you that they have chosen this book as your other teacher for the course.

Researching an assignment is different though. In this case you need to do some quick evaluation. Whether it is a book or an essay, figure out what it is about or you will end up wasting time reading it, only to learn you shouldn't have bothered. If it is a journal article, many have an abstract (i.e. a summary of the contents) at the beginning. There are also databases that abstract articles for you (ask your librarian). If it is a book, find a book review online. If you can't find an abstract or book review, then you need to do a superficial review by reading the introduction and conclusion.

Once you have done this, it is time to decide if it is worth reading more. Keeping your topic in mind, decide if it is:

1. Not worth any more time because it does not speak toward your topic.
2. Worth more of your time. The item may be somewhat related to your topic and you need to spend some time with it. Decide how much time, and seek to understand what the author is trying to convince you of, and the points that lead to their conclusion.

3. Worth a full front-to-back read. This is a major decision because it is a time commitment, and you need to jealously guard your time. If something is right on topic, read it well. (Just a tip: when you are researching to write an essay, there are few, if any, few full books that are worth a full front-to-back read).

Take Notes, Highlight, Understand

If you are not taking notes while researching and reading in college, you are not doing it right. Decide a note-taking system that is right for you (see the Tools chapter) and use it. Notes are a mental system for jogging your memory to remember what you read. More than just highlighting and note-taking, aim also for understanding. In 30 seconds, can you describe the purpose of the essay or chapter you just read? What are the main points, and what conclusion was drawn? For every article, essay, book chapter, and book you read, write a 1 paragraph summary of it for yourself. If you can do this, you are reading with understanding.

Be Patient With Yourself

Yes I know you've been reading since you were in grade 1, but you are in a whole new world now. And just like the frustration a 5-year old has when reading, you'll struggle at times when reading at an academic level. You'll come across words you've never seen before (hint: use a dictionary!), and there will be times when you read a page over and over again because you just don't understand it.

That's OKAY.

You are entering into various fields of study, and your professor and the writers you read all went through the same process. They had to learn new, specialized vocabulary too. Like almost every new skill you've ever acquired in your life, reading for knowledge is a skill that you will develop over time. And like every new skill you've acquired, you got better with practice, by not giving up, by WANTING to get better, and by cutting yourself some slack during the learning process. The fact that you are reading a book like this means you have the fortitude to do it.

Chapter 10: Crush IT at Writing a Great Paper
Bryan Tinlin

If you struggle with writing college/university papers you are not alone. Like almost every other student I've encountered, you likely fall into one or more of the following five categories:

1. You lack Confidence About Writing
   - Student: I don't like writing because it's not my strength.
   - Advisor: You lack confidence and haven't been properly encouraged.
2. You feel overwhelmed.
   - Student: I often procrastinate because I don't know where to start.
   - Advisor: You are overwhelmed or lack interest in the subject.
3. You haven't been taught how to write an academic paper.
   - Student: I put lots of effort into my papers and I still receive low grades.
   - Advisor: You firmly believe or have been taught that effort on its own is enough to deserve a good grade.
4. You didn't understand that writing is a skill not just something you're born with.
   - Student: "I know what I want to say but I just can't get it on paper."
   - Advisor: Putting your thoughts on paper is a skill that you need to develop, not something you're

born with. There's nothing wrong with you, you just need to practice and get help.

5. You didn't understand what research has to do with writing a paper.
   - Student: I can't get anything out. I often suffer from writer's block.
   - Advisor: You haven't developed research skills. It's hard to know what to write until you've conducted some preliminary research into the topic.

Keep these core struggles in mind as I share with you how to write a great paper. Before I go any further, I want to assure you that you are not alone. When I was an undergraduate student I was a very poor writer and could identify with all five categories. I soon realized that I had a choice: give up or take charge. I decided to take charge and get help.

My grades eventually improved over the years, but it took time. Even in graduate studies I frequently consulted a writing tutor. I had to humble myself and admit I needed help. I decided that if I wanted my financial investment to pay off I had to do something about my writing. The same professor who gave me a D on my first paper complemented me three years later on my 80 page thesis.

Why is writing so important? In a nutshell, if you learn to write well it will make a huge difference in your professional career. Even if you don't plan on becoming a professional writer, trust me when I tell you that writing will greatly influence how your employer views the quality of your work. The truth is that a professional cannot escape writing. And it is a mistake to think essay writing is only about the writing—it is also teaching you highly transferable skills like communication, argumentation, research, etc. Now is the time to learn to do it well.

If you need an example of how poor writing can affect someone's career, here is a clear example. I once walked into a newly renovated nation-wide fast-food chain and saw the following on the door:

NO PETS
NO SHOES
NO SHIRTS REQUIRED!

Do you think that someone on the writing team was having a bad day or that they hired someone who didn't know how to write? I wonder now how much that mistake cost the company. Imagine if you were the one who wrote that message. How would it reflect on your integrity as a professional in the marketing department?

10 Steps to Help You Become a Solid Writer

Step 1: Ask a Great Writer How They Learned to be a Great Writer

There's no better way to learn how to be a great writer than to talk to one yourself. That's not to say there is a formula for creativity but there are intentional strategies you can employ that are common to all great writers. So go ahead and ask a great writer what strategies they use. If you aren't sure you know any great writers, ask your professor to refer a senior student you can talk to.

Step 2: Start Assignments Early

This has been mentioned before but bears repeating— Starting early is one of the keys to putting yourself on a track for writing success (see the chapter on scheduling for more help on this). Since most professors are required to provide you a course outline (or syllabus) on the first day of class, you have months to plan in advance of the paper deadline.

The benefits of starting early cannot be stressed enough. Here are just three of them:

1. You avoid cramming and the guilt and stress associated with it. That in itself is worth its weight in gold. If you value your health and mental well being, not to mention your academic record, you will start early.

2. A creative mind needs time. You may not think you have a creative mind but that's probably because you've haven't given yourself enough time to be creative. By planting your essay topic in your head, you've given your subconscious an opportunity to work all the time – on the bus, at your parent's house, in the shower, eating dinner, doing the laundry or just zoning out. Best of all,

when those ideas come to you, all you have to do is jot them down.

3. Giving yourself time means you have plenty of opportunity to rework, restructure and revise. Not to mention that you can afford to forgo writing on those days when you lack a great ideas. Remember, writing is a process. It takes time!

Step 3: Learn How to Research

This is one of the important skills mentioned in the Skills chapter. You'll quickly learn that, unlike high school, university and college professors are less interested in your opinions and more interested in what the research or experts in the subject matter have to say. The person grading your paper cares about research.

Remember that like writing, research is a skill. It takes time. Case in point: librarians have a master's degree in library sciences. That means beyond their first degree they spent an additional two years learning how to discern, locate, and use information in the library. The point is that you must do everything you can to develop your research skills. Here is how:

- Take advantage of library research seminars. This may sound as exciting as learning how to type properly, but trust me when I say that it will pay off handsomely in the end.
- Trust your librarian. Your librarian has years of education and a wealth of experience behind

them. Seek help from them regularly. That's why you pay tuition.

- Practice, practice, practice. The more time you invest in developing your research skills the better your papers will become. Good research skills can make the difference between a C paper and an A paper.
- Avoid cheating! Cheating or plagiarism is one of the most pervasive and damaging things you could possibly do to your academic career. Cheating at college is the equivalent of telling off your boss when you've had a bad day. The penalty for cheating, intentionally or unintentionally, can be very serious and could include academic dismissal. It can ruin your future plans. If you learn how to research properly and give credit to your academic sources, you are automatically learning how to avoid cheating.

Step 4: Act Like A Writer

What you read and how you speak influences your writing. I don't need to tell you that technology is changing how we write. Instant messaging, texting, and email are but a few of the culprits. If you want to be a good writer then read, read, read. Better yet, complete all of your required assigned readings. The more you practice, the better writer you will become. As you write, try to imitate the sound and tone of assigned readings for the course. Here are a few simple tips to follow:

- As painful as you think it may be, take the time to write full sentences in all your communication, especially by email. It won't be painful after a while and your readers, whomever that may be, will never be confused with what you are saying.
- Speak as you write. Don't be a sloppy speaker if you are trying to improve your writing.
- Edit, edit, edit. Did you know that your professors go through an editing process when they write their research papers? Take the time to edit what you write. There's nothing worse to a reader than guessing what you are trying to say. Finishing your essay a few days early, getting some distance from it, and then going back to edit it will reveal a lot of mistakes. Finally, find a peer who writes well and will edit your essays, and reciprocate the favor.

Step 5: Check With Your Professor to Make Sure You Are on The Right Track

Almost every student I've ever met failed to visit their professor or teaching assistant for feedback on their papers. Examples of common feedback from professors and teaching assistants include:

- Your argument is too broad. You are covering three topics in one. Pick one.
- Your thesis statement or research question is unclear. I'm not quite sure what you are trying to say.
- Your grammar and sentence structure needs work. You need help.

- Your research is too thin. I would recommend expanding the number and quality of your academic sources.
- Magazines and novels are not considered academic sources unless specifically expressed by your professor.

I would also suggest you check with your professors or teaching assistants (TA) at each of the writing steps:

- After you have chosen a topic and have formed an introductory outline
- After you have conducted preliminary research in the library
- After your first draft
- After your second draft

Aim to follow this process for at least your first year. If your professor or his TA doesn't want to see you that often, then consult with a tutor at the writing service or hire a writing tutor. In the end, your paper must make sense. Anyone should be able to read it and understand it regardless of the topic. Think of it this way: would a friend who isn't in the class—or isn't even in college— understand your essay? If not...revise and rewrite.

Don't be afraid to ask your professor for an example paper or for clarification if the description of the assignment is vague or unclear. If an assignment is unclear on the syllabus and you wait until the week before it is due to ask for clarification, the fault lies with you, and your professor will be unimpressed (and might not have time for you!).

Step 6: Get Help With Your Writing

Writing is no different than any other skill. The more you practice the better your writing will get. Having said that, you need to be intentional on how to become a better writer. Continuing to write in the same way won't yield better results. I would suggest you either book regular sessions with your writing tutorial service or plan to invest in a writing tutor. For students in the liberal arts or sciences, a writing tutor is equivalent to a math tutor for engineering students. That's how serious your professors take writing. Seek out someone who is not only an outstanding writer but can teach as well.

Step 7. Refine, Refine, Refine

Reworking and editing your paper is a process. It takes time, a lot of time. It is unrealistic to expect to hand in a refined piece of work if you haven't spent copious amounts of time on it. If your goal is to hand in something with excellence stamped on it then be prepared to invest everything you have in it. To a large degree, the final product will be a reflection of your effort particularly if you have followed all the other suggestions made in this chapter.

Step 8. Finish Early

Imagine handing in your paper on time or even early. What would that look like? You will avoid any penalties for tardiness, you will reduce your stress, and most importantly you will feel good about a job well done! Even better, if you are done early, find one more person to read it and offer edits and suggestions. Another pair of eyes will always catch things you miss. Even the highest paid and most famous authors in the world have editors—how much more will you!

Step 9. Get Feedback From the Grader

Feedback is crucial to becoming a better writer so take the time to learn from your mistakes. Some professors are better than others at offering feedback on your paper, so be bold and ask. Stick a post-it on the front of the paper saying:

"Dear Dr. Smith, Could I ask that you (or your marker) please offer me as much feedback as you can on every aspect of my essay. I want to learn from my mistakes so please be critical. Thanks very much for your assistance."

After handing in your paper ensure you book a time with your professor to go over what you did well and where you need improvement. This feedback will be an invaluable source of information that you can take with you to your next writing project. If the teacher cannot meet, then ask if their TA can go over it with you. If that can't happen, then take your essay to your writing tutor or the college writing centre and go over all of the feedback you received.

You won't need to do this for every assignment, but do it as much as possible as you enter into your education. Soon, you will be the tutor.

Step 10. Be Humble and Teachable

The trick to excelling at anything is to be humble. Most students come to college and university expecting to achieve great results on their papers. There are three reasons for this. First, some students did well in high school and expect to do as well in university or college. Second, many students have an attitude of entitlement (they worked hard so therefore they deserve a high grade). Third, some students believe they already know how to write and that their professor does not. The truth is that, 1) the writing expectations are generally much higher in university, 2) working hard in the wrong direction on an assignment doesn't deserve a good grade, and 3) your professor can write circles around you!

If you are humble then you are automatically teachable. By following this simple tip you will avoid the frustration, anger, and resentment that accompanies prideful students who believe that they are in the right and everyone else is in the wrong. I know I was guilty of that and I had to humble myself before I could really learn to write.

Investing in your writing is worth the time and the money. I can't say enough about how important writing is to your academic career and your professional career beyond your studies. It will impact your life in a positive way for years to come.

Chapter 11: Crush IT with Productivity
Danny Zacharias

Productive people are hard working and have structure in their lives. If you aren't this type of person, now is the time to start—you can BECOME a productive person. Creating productive and healthy habits will not only help you excel in your studies, but will make you the kind of person who influences others and who companies want to hire in the future. Some of this chapter may be repetitive, as many of these tips are important for succeeding in other previously discussed areas.

1. Eat well, exercise, and SLEEP
You know you need to eat well, so don't live off of pizza pops and cola. And if you are eating in a cafeteria make wise choices—there are salad bars in every cafeteria! Your brain needs good food. You aren't a tweenager anymore where it was fun to consume as much candy as possible. You are entering adulthood now and you are making your own choices. So make good food choices. Students also think it is "collegy" to start being a coffee addict, or to chug energy drinks late at night to stay up. It isn't cool; it's stupid. You know how much is too much, so be self-disciplined and choose water to stay hydrated instead of cola.

You also need to exercise, because your body will perform better the more you move. If you move slowly, so does your mind—it is as simple as that. Schedule exercise into your routine. There is so much opportunity in higher education to join intramural teams, use the gym, do sports with other students, etc., that you have zero excuse. And even if all of these things are not available, you still have no excuse. I exercise several times a week in my living room or office with no equipment. Body weight exercises (like Turbulence training[1]) and Yoga (check out DDP Yoga[2] for example) can be done even in small dorm rooms.

Finally, there isn't a college rule that says all students should sleep as little as possible! If you aren't in bed between 11-12 each night and getting 6-8 hours of sleep, you better start rethinking why you came to university— to party or to learn. (And if you follow the suggestion for managing homework, you won't have any reason to stay up late doing assignments either!)

Another sleep tip—some companies and numerous productivity gurus are increasingly recommending naps. I frequently nap in my office. And if you are the kind of person that can put your head on the desk in the library and clonk out for a bit, start doing it! Naps re-energize your mind. The key to a good nap is the length—if you nap more than 20-25 minutes you will enter into a deeper sleep cycle and feel groggy when you wake up instead of refreshed. Set your iPod alarm for 20 minutes, and practice the art of the siesta!

---

[1] www.tiny.cc/TurbulenceExercise

[2] www.ddpyoga.com

2. Practice Rest

While Christians and Jews are familiar with the practice of Sabbath rest (even if they don't actually do it!), the idea of a consistent time of "no-work" during the week is good for everyone. There are cycles and seasons of life and by and large college study means little leisure time. Still, if your schedule allows it (and if you've disciplined yourself to stick to your schedule), you should try and take a day or half of a day off from school work each week. During these times, do the things you love to do: watch a movie, paint, knit, read comics, play a board game, take a hike. Just get your mind off assignments for a little while.

3. This is Your Job, Treat It As Such

If you are in university or college, IT IS YOUR FULLTIME JOB. Treat it that way. Don't sleep in just because your class starts in the afternoon that day. Get up early (get up the same time every day), get ready for your day, and get to it! If you are not in class, you should be doing work in your dorm or in the library. If you keep at this pace, you'll start to notice that your evenings will be free much more often. You will also find that while your fellow students are cramming, pulling all-nighters, or begging for extensions, you'll be heading to the movies to see the latest blockbuster because you managed your life well through the whole semester. In my graduate years there were a few semesters when I was completely done my coursework (minus exams) when my peers were just starting their major assignments—it was a GREAT feeling.

4. Take Short Breaks

Did you know that the most productive people are NOT those who glue themselves to their desk for hours on end? The most productive people hit their work HARD for chunks of time, and then take breaks in between. I personally follow a 55-minute work, 5-minute break routine in my office. Some people, like professional musicians, will do 90-minutes of hard work followed by 15-minutes of break.

Have you ever had a deadline that you were working on, when all of a sudden some sort of setback or tragedy hits and it takes a huge chunk of time away from you? I have had this happen to me many times. If you were like me, many of those times you were still able to make your deadline. How is that possible? It is because circumstances forced you to focus in like a laser on finishing the task at hand. Everything else was shut out and you locked in to your task to make that deadline.

What does this have to do with taking breaks? Choosing this type of disciplined scheduling is essentially a mind-hack that taps into your ability to focus yourself and achieve amazing productivity: you are forcing yourself to work hard and fast to get the reward of a break—you are setting yourself mini-deadlines through the day. If you do this type of disciplined scheduling, you will begin to challenge yourself to get certain amounts done before your break comes. In efforts to hit these mini-targets, you will force yourself to focus and not be distracted.

I challenge you to try to schedule your homework time. Use an alarm on your computer to mark the times. If you use a Mac, you can use the program I use called BreakTime.[3]

5. Be Your Own TaskMaster

No one can make you succeed but you. If you want to be productive, that is a choice you make. To stop procrastination and move into the realm of productivity, make sure you are in charge of every single minute of your day. Make the choice to wake up early. Make the choice to say no to time-wasters. Tell yourself what to do, then do it. Be hard on yourself by evaluating how you are spending your time. Take the time to do an honest evaluation of your day(s) and see if you wasted time on unimportant things. Focus in on quality and productivity, and force the lazy part of yourself into submission under the one who wants to Crush IT.

6. Get Some Distance from Minor and Major Assignments

You know as well as I do that your best work on a major project is not at 3am, 6 hours before it is due. Try and finish major assignments 5-7 days early and your minor assignments a day or two early. This gives you a chance to step away from it and then come back for a final proofread and edit. If you start this practice you'll soon recognize how valuable it is because you'll catch all sorts

---

[3] www.tiny.cc/BreakTimeApp

of mistakes. It can also give you time to practice those writing tips provided.

Planning and working ahead by following the suggested scheduling practice allows you to work in the zone of quality and productivity. Steve Covey is a famous author who wrote *The 7 Habits of Highly Effective People.* In that book, he identified 4 quadrants of work: 1) important & urgent, 2) important but not urgent, 3) urgent but not important, 4) not important and not urgent. You will be at your most productive and produce the best quality work when you are in quadrant 2. The reality is that most students are in quadrant 1 because they have not scheduled and planned ahead for their assignments. And the reason that they end up in quadrant 1 at the end of the semester is because they have spent too much of their time in quadrant 4. You can guess what quadrant 4 looks like, but here is our sketch of it.

The 4 Quadrants for Students

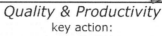

	URGENT	NOT URGENT
IMPORTANT	*Necessity* key action: **MANAGE** ~ Personal Crises ~ All deadlines 2 days or less away ~ Legitimate Emergency ~ Pressing technical problems (i.e. computer blew up)	*Quality & Productivity* key action: **FOCUS** ~ Required week's reading ~ Small weekly assignments ~ Major upcoming assignments ~ Improving student skills ~ Exercising
NOT IMPORTANT	*Others' Priorities* key action: **USE CAUTION** ~ Teaching others how to use their computer/ software ~ Some emails/calls ~ Any urgency masquerading as importance	*Time Waste* key action: **AVOID** ~ mindless Netflix/ TV/YouTube watching ~ Most Facebook/ Twitter ~ Gaming ~ Some emails ~ Some calls

adaptation of Stephen Covey's 4 Quadrants, *7 Habits of Highly Effective People* (2004)

7. Know What Kind of Learner You Are (and tap into it!)

I'm surprised how many students don't know what kind of learner they are, or if they do, how they do not tap into that knowledge. For instance, if you are an auditory learner, I'd consider (with permission) audio recording lectures to listen over again (use the notebook feature of MS Word, an app like Notability[4] on the iPad, or the LiveScribe SmartPen[5] mentioned previously). Auditory learners should also be reading out loud to themselves or getting their texts as audiobooks. If you're a kinesthetic learner, sitting at a desk will drive you crazy. Try walking around while reading instead. To understand what kind of learner you are and some additional tips for working with your learning style, check out the Education Planner[6] or About Learning[7] website.

8. Invest Time And Smarts Into Your Marks

I defined major assignments as those that have large marks associated with them. But you also need to actually make sure you are doing things correctly. If your syllabus is fuzzy on what exactly a teacher is looking for, get clarification right away. Also ask around and find out about your teacher's marking style. If your teacher moonlights on the grammar police squad, then put extra time into that. If they like very specific types of footnotes, then invest time into that. Don't be afraid to ask your professor for example papers, and keep asking until you get it. Also, determine how much weight is put on class participation. If it is significant, then you need to break past that shyness and engage in class.

---

[4] www.tiny.cc/notability

[5] www.tiny.cc/LivescribeSmartpen

[6] www.educationplanner.org

[7] www.aboutlearning.com

9. Find a Like-minded Peer

Find someone who will sit with you in the library—not to distract you but so you can push each other towards excellence. Even introverts like having someone they know close by, even if words aren't exchanged. Also, agree to edit each other's major assignments. A peer will really help you see when your writing is unclear.

10. Choose to Turn Off Distractors

In the effort to be engaged online we often make ourselves immediately available and always ready to be interrupted. The secret of productive people is they know how to set themselves up for distraction-free work. There are precious few times when there are actual emergencies that require your immediate attention. Here are some simple ways to stop distracting yourself:

- Several software items were mentioned in the third chapter which can help you not be distracted by the internet and social media.
- If you don't have the strength to cancel your Facebook account, at least turn off the notifications so that you are not getting emails and updates on your mobile device every few minutes.
- If you are on Twitter, disable those updates.
- If you use a Mac, turn off Notification Center. Same for your mobile device.
- There is no rule that your email program must check for new email every 30 seconds! Change the settings so email is checked only when you hit the "receive" button.

- Hide your mobile device in your bag so you don't see it every time it lights up.
- If you have a cell phone, turn the ringer off.

11. Back Up Your Work

Only once have I had a completed essay totally disappear on me—what an awful feeling! If you are not safe-guarding yourself by backing up your work regularly you will at some point end up doing assignments all over again. Talk about unproductive!

Fortunately, there are some ultra-simple ways to protect yourself. The simplest is to install free cloud storage apps like Dropbox[8] or SugarSync.[9] Sign up for your account, download and install the program, and you will have a folder on your computer that will be backed up to the cloud. EVERY major thing I work on is saved to one of my cloud services.

You are investing time and money into your education. Honor those investments and take it seriously. While most of your peers are partying and procrastinating, Crush IT by being productive.

----

[8] www.tiny.cc/DropBox4u

[9] www.tiny.cc/SugarSync4u

Appendix: Wiping Your Grades – What to do in the event of exceptional personal circumstances
Bryan Tinlin

I want to share with you something that very few students hear about until they actually need it. I'm talking about an academic appeal, something you hope you are never in a position to need. But should the situation arise, I want you to benefit from my experience working on the inside of the university system for many years. This knowledge will equip you with the information you will need to successfully submit your appeal.

Each year, thousands of young people set out to pursue college and university studies with every intention of doing well. For some of these students, despite their best efforts, life throws them a curve ball. I'm not talking about the everyday life challenges like a strained relationship with your boyfriend or girlfriend or when your car breaks down on the way to school or the regret you had by taking on a much heavier course load than you should have. Instead, I'm referring to those exceptional circumstances that are beyond your control and have significant impact on your overall academic performance.

What constitutes exceptional? Here are a few examples:

1. lengthy illness that incapacitates you for an extended period of time

2. recently diagnosed or recurrent illness
3. death in your immediate family
4. unexpected and grave financial problem (i.e theft of household belongings or loss of your house in a fire)
5. unexpected surgery
6. relapse from a diagnosed addiction or compulsive behavior (gambling, alcohol, drugs, to name a few)
7. recently diagnosed learning disability
8. harm that was done to you (i.e. an assault)
9. other traumatic event

If you can identify with any of these examples you should investigate the academic appeal process at your college or university. Most institutions allow students who have experienced such exceptional circumstances to submit an appeal. Although the rules and regulations vary institution to institution, generally speaking there are common guidelines that each of them subscribes to.

Common Questions About Academic Appeals

What if I am afraid to submit an appeal?

The number one reason why many students choose not to submit a petition is that they are afraid that they will have to relive what happened. My advice is to get help for the issue before submitting a petition. Dealing with the pain is the right thing to do. As hard as it may be, if you don't deal with the pain now it will spring back up in your life sooner or later. Your emotional well-being—self-care—should be one of the top priorities ALWAYS. Seeking help is also a step toward getting the necessary professional documentation you will need to support your appeal.

What would I be appealing?

Although this sounds like a silly question it is a very common question. An academic appeal is a request to wipe your grades from your record. Having said that, most institutions do not allow you to pick and choose which course(s) will be wiped. That is called 'selective withdrawal' and it is rarely given because your institution does not want to set a precedent. If such as precedent was established, every student would ask for the low grades to be withdrawn and the good grades to be left on their permanent academic record (known as your transcript).

Instead, you must decide two things:

1. Whether you want to proceed with an academic appeal.
2. If you do decide to proceed, which academic term(s) you would like to request grades to be wiped from your record.

For some students this an easy decision because they achieved consistently poor grades in all courses because of their exceptional circumstance. For other students it isn't an easy decision. You may have A grades mixed in with C+ and F grades. I recommend you keep in mind that this may be your one and only opportunity to wipe your record clean. This is particularly relevant for students who intend to apply to professional schools like law or medicine, where presenting an impeccable record is critical to successful admission.

Keep in mind that the time frame indicated on your supporting documentation must be consistent with the time frame for the academic term(s) you are requesting to be withdrawn from your record. It is difficult to expect a committee to honour your request to have grades withdrawn from your record from fall 2013 when your doctor's note indicates you were hospitalized in winter 2014.

Is there a cost to appeal my case?

Generally the answer is no. Your tuition covers this service. Having said that, it is worth checking with your registrar's office or the administrative office responsible for handling the appeals. Some institutions charge for certain registrarial services in order to curb the volume of submissions and to discourage flagrant abuse. At the institution where I worked they didn't charge for an academic petition but they did charge for other services.

What do I need to present to the appeal committee?

You need independent certifiable documentation that supports your claim. Medical notes from a medical doctor, health care practitioner, or professional counselor are the most common forms of supporting documentation since health issues account for the majority of all petitions.

The key is that the person submitting the documentation has to be independent (i.e. not your mom or dad) and professionally accredited.

I haven't sought professional help for my issue. I don't have any documentation. Can I still submit an appeal?

This is tricky one. Although your institution may say it is too late to go back to a professional, I would encourage you to go ahead anyway. Many people don't make objective decisions when traumatic things happen to them. Go to your professional counselor or medical doctor and speak with them about your issue. It's a good way to get help and at the same time request supporting documentation from them. The only advice I would add is that you go to the professional first and foremost for help and only secondarily for documentation. Some professionals will refuse to issue you a note particularly when you haven't fully divulged to them what happened and how it affected you. Seeking help becomes even more important for those universities or college that require the medical professional to complete a 'fit to return' form. This form indicates to the institution when you are able to return to academic studies. The point I'm making is that seeking out help has many benefits, the least of which is acquiring the necessary documentation you need to submit an appeal.

Can I request a withdrawal for more than one academic term?

Generally speaking yes. You can request to go back many terms. In some cases I've seen two years withdrawn from a student's record. It goes without saying that all grades earned, both good and bad, are completely wiped from your record.

Is there a time limit on how far I can go back?

In general it is best to deal with the matter as soon as possible. The longer you wait the less likely your request will be granted. Having said that, you have nothing to lose by submitting your request other than the time it takes you to complete the appeal.

Do I have to meet with the appeal committee in person?

Generally speaking no. This is particularly true for medium to large-sized institutions. They don't have the resources to hear a student's testimony. The other reason that committees are not keen to meet with students is because of the sensitive nature of some of the cases and the traumatic impact that the issue has had on the student.

Can I get someone to review my appeal?

Generally speaking no. Internally, we call this 'coaching'. 'Coaching' is a process that uses an insider's institutional knowledge to improve your chance of getting a favourable outcome. In short it is cheating.

Besides, no one wants the responsibility of interfering or biasing your personal testimony. It's your testimony and no one else's.

How should I outline my appeal?

I advise students to use the following format:

1. describe what happened
2. when it happened
3. the professional counsel you sought out
4. attach the documentation you are presenting

Avoid writing a novel and instead be sure to include enough information that your appeal is complete and it makes sense.

Can I request a financial refund at the same time?

Yes. Keep in mind that the academic appeals committee and the financial appeals committee are often separate bodies. Therefore it is possible to have a successful academic appeal but not have a successful financial appeal. Institutions are very reluctant to refund your money. They normally work under the premise that you paid for services that were ultimately delivered. Having said that it still doesn't hurt to try and argue your case and request a tuition reimbursement.

The decision. What will the committee be looking for?

Committee members consider a number of variables when reviewing your petition. Here are a few of them:

1. Do you have a history of submitting academic appeals?
2. The integrity of your record.
3. The circumstance of the issue you are appealing and the degree to which the issue was truly beyond your control.
4. The quality and source of your supporting documentation.
5. Your fit to return documentation, if applicable.
6. Your responsibility in the matter, if applicable.
7. Whether or not you could have dropped the courses in question prior to the academic drop deadline thus avoiding the need to submit an academic appeal.

Final Words of Wisdom

The decision to submit a petition is a personal one. However, if you do decide to submit a petition, ensure that aside from the petition itself you get help for the issue that brought you to this point.

BONUS OFFER

We hope you enjoyed reading Crush IT at College. We want to see you succeed and we sincerely hope that this book has armed you with the knowledge and skills to Crush IT at college or university.

I (Bryan Tinlin) want to make a special offer to those of you who have purchased this book. If you still feel you need some coaching, or if you are trying to decide if college/university is the right choice for you and need some counsel, or even if you are a parent seeking to help your child, I offer one-on-one sessions at AcademicAdviceOnline.com.

Book a Skype session with me and use this special link for 25% off the regular cost:

AcademicAdviceOnline.com/promotion
Password: ebookbonus

Because I appreciate you purchasing this book, please feel free to give this unique link to someone else if you don't feel you are going to use it.

Now, go Crush IT!

TERMS OF SERVICE

These terms of service contain important information, including warranty disclaimers and limitations of liability.

1. Information of a general nature only and no warranties provided. The information provided in this book is for general information purposes only. The information in this book **should be regarded as suggestions and not professional advice, including legal or medical advice**. Ultimately, decisions relating to the education of a client are the clients to make. The authors do not give any express or implied warranties and make no representations in relation to this book. Information in this book should not be relied upon without first validating the information from appropriate sources and obtaining professional advice, including medical or legal, where it is prudent to do so. You should make and rely upon your own assessments and enquires to verify the accuracy or prudence of the information that is provided.

2. Limitation of liability

The authors shall not be responsible for any loss, damage, claim, cost or expense whatsoever arising out of or in connection with these terms received.

3. Bonus Offer disclaimer

The bonus offer contained in this book is valid while advising services of Tinlin Academic Advising and Consulting are available from www.academicadviceonline.com.

19328422R00061

Made in the USA
Charleston, SC
18 May 2013